I0568573

Wicca

A Beginner's Guide to Wiccan Magick

Sarah Rhodes

© **Rivercat Books LLC Copyright 2022 - All rights reserved.**

The content contained within this book may not be reproduced, duplicated or transmitted without direct written permission from the author or the publisher.

Under no circumstances will any blame or legal responsibility be held against the publisher, or author, for any damages, reparation, or monetary loss due to the information contained within this book, either directly or indirectly.

Legal Notice:

This book is copyright protected. It is only for personal use. You cannot amend, distribute, sell, use, quote or paraphrase any part, or the content within this book, without the consent of the author or publisher.

Disclaimer Notice:

Please note the information contained within this document is for educational and entertainment purposes only. All effort has been executed to present accurate, up to date, reliable, complete information. No warranties of any kind are declared or implied. Readers acknowledge that the author is not engaged in the rendering of legal, financial, medical or professional advice. The content within this book has been derived from various sources. Please consult a licensed professional before attempting any techniques outlined in this book.

By reading this document, the reader agrees that under no circumstances is the author responsible for any losses, direct or indirect, that are incurred as a result of the use of the information contained within this document, including, but not limited to, errors, omissions, or inaccuracies.

Table of Contents

Introduction: Why Wicca?

If you're reading this book, the likelihood is you have some interest in Wicca. You're probably considering giving it a go because maybe somebody you know is a Wiccan, and you want to know more, or maybe you just like learning about new things. Whatever the case, this book is the right place to start.

Wicca is a wonderful Pagan religion that, in its most basic form, is all about celebrating the natural world that we inhabit. However, as the result of some unfortunate misrepresentation, it can sometimes come with negative connotations. When a person hears the phrase "I am a witch," it's not uncommon that the first thing they think of is a circle of witches praising the devil or a group of teen girls performing evil rituals to curse an ex-boyfriend. Some witches might do those things, and hey, to each their own. However, those witches are not Wiccans.

The word 'witch' can be a bit contentious for some Wiccans. For the purposes of this book, we welcome all 'w'-words. Wiccan, witch, witch-adjacent, wonderful person. If you want to learn about Wicca and witchcraft because you grew up watching shows like *Charmed* and *Sabrina the Teenage Witch,* that's great. If you read about ancient Celts and want to learn more about their religious beliefs, fantastic. If you want to learn how to perform a money spell, that's okay too. Wicca is a personal journey, and you don't need to justify your reasons for learning and practicing to anyone. As long as your intentions are good, you can practice for whatever reasons you like.

Speaking of teenage witches, there has been some change in the image related to the word 'Wiccan.' Some people have realized that Wiccans are not scary old ladies with pointy noses and have moved on to a more contemporary image of magickal ladies. The kind that wear flowy skirts and have their belly buttons pierced. From the Halliwell sisters and their Book of Shadows to Buffy and Willow using witchcraft to rid the world of vampires, young and stylish witches were all the rage in the 1990s and 2000s. While this is definitely a change in the perception from evil old ladies, it is not much of an improvement in terms of accuracy.

Wiccans come in all shapes, sizes, genders, and interests. They make different life and style choices, and they are all valid in their practice. Since Wicca is not an organized religion—that is, there is no one single leader or sacred text—there is no unified idea of who can and does practice the craft. This means that all Wiccans can choose to present themselves differently from one another, and they can choose to practice in different ways. Some practice alone, some with a coven. Some practice publicly, others privately. Some choose to express Wicca through their fashion, some through their art, and some in their home. It's all personal. Of course, there are guidelines and suggestions within the religion that will help people to make these decisions.

Benefits of Wicca

Practicing Wicca—in any capacity—has loads of different benefits that can have a positive impact on several aspects of your life. In general, there are many benefits to exploring spirituality of any kind, and Wicca is an easy and enjoyable way to reap those benefits.

One overall benefit that comes along pretty early on when practicing Wicca is an improvement of one's mental well-being.

Mindfulness, relaxation, and meditation are a big part of Wiccan ritual and practice that can obviously do wonders for your mood and overall state of being. Taking some time out of your day to meditate and focus on your practice can be a great way to shake off any tension taking over your body or negative thoughts creeping into your brain. If you're having a particularly bad time, having a distraction or a task to focus on can take your mind away from whatever is causing you stress or sadness.

In a similar vein, practicing Wicca is the perfect excuse to go outside and explore your natural surroundings in whatever form they take. Disconnect from technology and reconnect with nature. Look for herbs or plants that you can use in your rituals, absorb the energy from the sun, and take in the fresh air. Wicca is all about expressing love for our natural world, something that can be easily forgotten in the hustle and bustle of everyday life. On top of that, engaging in any sort of ritual practice that calls for some level of planning is a great way to give some structure to your day. Having a daily routine—as simple as lighting a candle as you begin your day or as complex as preparing an offering to the Lord and the Lady following some meditation at sunrise—will give you a sense of stability and structure.

The performative aspect of spell casting and ritual working can serve as a major confidence booster. When you are performing a ritual or reciting a spell, you are in control, something that perhaps you don't get to experience much in other aspects of your life. The need to speak out loud during rituals is great practice for public speaking, and as you communicate with your deities, you can practice your general communication skills for life outside of the altar. If you don't often find yourself controlling the flow of conversations in your daily life, you can really take this time to push yourself to feel in charge. Of course, you must be wary of becoming too comfortable with power. As with all things in Wicca (and in life), be sure to find the balance.

The creative aspect of Wicca is a great way to flex your artistic muscles and find new ways to express your individuality. From creative writing in spell work, interior design when setting up your altar, drawing inside your Book of Shadows, or using the craft to inspire your personal aesthetic, there is so much creative potential that you can tap into when forming your personal practice.

Introducing Wicca into your life comes with a supportive community of other people practicing this religion. Whether you find them in person or online, your fellow Wiccans will be there to guide and support you through your practice and your struggles. Finally, the Threefold Law, which we will talk about in Chapter 2, is a great reason to practice kindness, calmness, and compassion in your everyday life.

These elements, plus many others, have an immeasurably positive effect on you and those around you, and they are just some of the benefits that come with introducing Wicca into your life.

What to Expect From This Book

We're going to cover a lot of ground in this book, but don't expect to come out at the end being able to predict the future or make an object float just by looking at it. Wiccan magick is a skill, and like any skill, it takes understanding and practice. This book will give you all the basic tools you need to get started.

The first two chapters will cover the most basic of basics: where, when, and how the religion started and the basic beliefs of Wicca. Chapter 3 will address some common misconceptions about the practice and aid you in busting some myths. Next, in Chapter 4, we will build up on these core elements and look closer at the many different ways that one could choose to practice Wicca.

Chapter 5 will break down key dates observed by Wiccans throughout the year, what these dates represent, and how you can use your faith to observe and celebrate these dates.

Finally, Chapters 6 and 7 will give you some practical information on how to carry your faith and practice further. We'll go over the many different tools used in Wiccan practice and ritual magick, the Book of Shadows (yes, *Charmed* got that bit right), and Wiccan altars. We'll also cover the key skills required to practice magick, such as visualization and grounding. If you're feeling up to it, you might even want to try your hand at a spell or ritual charm.

Above all, you can expect to step away from this book having a clear understanding of Wiccan beliefs and Wiccan magick. Let us begin.

An ye harm none, do what ye will.

Chapter 1: Origins

When talking about the origins of Wicca—the how, when, why, and so on—you will sometimes find people who say it is a practice that goes back centuries. Other times, people will say that it only started in the 20th century. So, which one is it?

The truth is that it's actually a little bit of both.

The base components of Wicca, such as the principal morals and magickal rituals, stem from religious beliefs and practices that go back thousands of years, well before Christianity was established as a religion (or even thought of, for that matter). However, Wicca as a structured and recognized religion only really began to grow legs in the late 19th and early 20th century when the British occult movement was gaining some traction. In fact, the word 'Wicca' was only invented in the mid-20th century.

However, before we get into the history of the religion, let us just clarify something. Not all witches are Wiccans, and not all Wiccans are witches. Witches existed before Wicca was established, and a person can be a witch but not subscribe to Wiccan ideals. There are also other Pagan religions that do not deal with witchcraft or magick of any kind. People sometimes use the words 'Wicca,' 'witch,' and 'Pagan' interchangeably, yet they are not the same thing. The word 'Wiccan' was in fact only coined in 1954. So, it is important to note that any study or mention of witchcraft before the middle of the 20th century is not directly related to Wicca. The two are linked, of course, but they are not the same.

We will go into a more detailed distinction between the denominations of witch and Wiccan later on in the book, but it is important to note that, before the 1950s, most people still thought about a witch as the "black magic, burn her at the stake" kind of person, and these witches did not all die out during the witch trials. Just keep that in mind as we go on. For the purposes of this book, a Wiccan is someone who practices the ritual of magick and subscribes to a set of key beliefs and philosophies, while a witch is someone who only practices magick.

Now, on to some history.

Well After the Middle Ages

Many people will attribute the organization of Wicca to a man called Gerald Gardner. While this is definitely true for the most part, the person who should probably be credited for the new modern interest in witchcraft is Dr. Margaret Murray, an Anglo-Indian anthropologist, Egyptologist, archeologist, folklorist, and historian. In 1921 Murray wrote *The Witch-Cult in Western Europe*, which was a study based on reports of the witchcraft trials. This is the first time that a scholar of note was looking at the subject of witchcraft with an unbiased eye. Up until this point, most work written on the subject seemed to subscribe to the early Christian belief that witchcraft in any form was a type of heresy. *The Witch-Cult in Western Europe* posited the idea that witchcraft wasn't actually a form of Christian heresy, but actually the practice of an old Pagan fertility cult that predated Christianity and survived the anti-Pagan purge of the Middle Ages. It was Murray's research that would give way to Gardner's interest in witchcraft.

In the 1940s, Gardner—now in his sixties and having lived an extremely well-traveled life—was studying the occult practices of the past and the present. For clarity's sake, the 'occult' here refers to "matters regarded as involving the action or influence of supernatural or supernormal powers or some secret knowledge of them". Following this new interest in witchcraft and the occult, Gardner found out that his step-grandmother—his grandfather's second wife—was known, at least by reputation, to be a witch, and he had an ancestor by the name of Gizell Gairdner who was burnt for being a witch in the year 1640. Using this familial link, Gardner was initiated into an existing coven in Christchurch, a town in the United Kingdom.

It is important to take a second here to acknowledge that covens and practicing witches were in existence before the time of Gardner, before that of Murray even. As we outlined before, witches have existed for centuries, and while the Christians attempted to squash the religion in the Middle Ages (all the way up until around 1750), the traditions and practices—rooted in folk magic—lived on. They simply moved underground. The traditions would be passed down by family members, and these practicing witches would be referred to as "fam trad witches." Fam trad witches continued to practice their craft into the 18th and 19th centuries and would be the basis of studies and research, such as that of Dr. Murray. So, covens of practicing witches may not have been a popular occurrence, but they would not have been impossible to locate.

At this point it was the mid-1940s, and Gardner felt very strongly that too many people still thought of witches as being devil-worshiping evil women. Although Dr. Murray's works had gained a decent amount of attention, they weren't exactly number one best-selling books. The general public wouldn't have been picking up *The Witch-Cult in Western Europe* for some easy bedtime reading. Gardner wanted everyone to know that witches aren't evil women or con artists, but actually a group of people with a deep respect for nature, tradition, and folklore.

However, at this time, the Witchcraft Act of 1735 was still in place. This was a British parliamentary bill that claimed that it was still a crime for someone to claim that they had magical powers, and those convicted would be sentenced to a maximum penalty of one year in jail. Therefore, it was no surprise that the rest of Gardner's coven wasn't too keen on the idea of letting everyone know what they were up to. His way around this was to write a historical novel called *High Magic's Aid* (published in 1949) that essentially explained everything that modern witches were up to, but it was framed as fiction. This was Gardner's tiptoe into the pool of magickal writing that would eventually lead to the organization of what we now call Wicca.

Special K

Speaking of magic, what's with the 'k'? The word 'magick' was coined by Aleister Crowley, another person who is key to the history of Wicca, but who is also quite problematic. Crowley was an English occultist, poet, and writer (amongst many other things), who coined the word 'magick' to distinguish his work from the sleight-of-hand tricks that stage magicians would use. Magick would indicate a true power that was obtained from the divine and the mystic, not illusion work. Although he did a lot of formidable work in the realm of mysticism and the occult, he also stood by some problematic beliefs. Crowley was known to be a misogynist and racist, and a lot of his work would lean toward Satanist tendencies. Gardner met Crowley in 1947, and Crowley's writings would have a great influence on Gardner's writings and later work in wiccan magick, with Gardner even including some of Crowley's rituals in his own practices.

Anyway, back to Gardner and his growing craft. Taking the things he had learned from Murray's writings, the practices he had picked up from his original coven, and the rituals and teachings he adopted from Crowley, Gardner began to string all of this into a new practice that he called Wicca. In 1951, the Witchcraft Act of 1735 was repealed, meaning there would no longer be any legal repercussions for anyone who claimed to be a witch (or were accused of being one). Gardner took this chance to promote the craft by writing two more books that were now presented as fact, not fiction. His practice was quickly termed Gardnerian Wicca and is a style of Wicca that is still practiced today. He also often spoke to the press about his work and appealed to the public to learn more about Wicca and witchcraft, emphasizing that it was not in any way an evil or Satanic practice. All this writing and talking with the press attracted the ire of fam trad witches. Not only did they oppose Gardner's pick-and-mix style of witchcraft—one that pulled together occult practices and folk traditions—but they were also unimpressed by his apparent want for attention.

The truth is that Gardner was 67 at this point, and many of his fellow witches and Wiccans were his age or older. He was worried that the new religion would die out with them and was desperately attempting to appeal to the younger crowds that might be interested in taking up the practice and keeping it going. It clearly worked, otherwise you wouldn't be reading this book right now.

Groovy, Baby

As Wicca gained popularity with younger people in Britain, it also traveled across the pond. Raymond Buckland is credited with taking Gardnerian Wicca over to the United States, along with his wife Rosemary. Buckland is an author and Wiccan who has written extensively on the topics of Wicca and witchcraft. In fact, if you are looking for a very detailed account on the history of witchcraft and how it evolved into Wicca, his book *Witchcraft from the Inside* is a highly suggested read. Buckland is originally from London, but just before they moved over to the US in 1962, they would become Gardner's first initiates to practice outside of the UK. Gardner would pass away two years later. The 1960s and 1970s saw Wicca grow in popularity among new Wiccans all over the world. The second wave feminists also had a lasting impact on the religion, making way for an increased focus on worshipping the Goddess and the divine feminine. Post-medieval religion—particularly Christianity—was very patriarchal, so an acknowledgement of a female deity was welcomed and encouraged. The 1970s also saw a rise in what is called "Eclectic Wicca," which saw Wiccans combine a mixture of rituals and beliefs from different practices to suit their own journey, much like what Gardner himself had done 20 years earlier. In fact, Gardnerian Wicca was falling slightly out of favor at this time, and different paths were slowly starting to form. We will discuss these different paths in a later chapter.

It wasn't all feminism and happiness though. As witchcraft and Wicca grew in both popularity and visibility, it attracted some unnecessary attention. Some of this attention came in the form of pop culture, as authors and directors included witchcraft more often in their work, sometimes without doing the adequate research. A good example of this is the book-turned-movie *Rosemary's Baby*, released in 1967 and 1968, respectively. In the story, Ira Levin included characters that identified as witches, yet the rituals they practiced were more akin to Satanic worship than actual witchcraft. Unfortunately, the book and movie did not accurately portray witchcraft, and this led to increased bad press for witches and Wiccans. This resulted in two things; the first is that some more unsavory characters began to identify as witches and Wiccans without subscribing to Wiccan beliefs, and the second is that Wiccans who were genuinely following the craft were again seen as evil-doers and devil-worshipers.

And Today?

Despite this, the Wiccan religion continued—and continues—to grow. By the end of the 20th century, several Wiccan churches and covens had been legally recognized as religious non-profit organizations. Wiccan priests and priestesses were present at institutions such as prisons, and more individuals would find enlightenment on their own path. The distinction between witches and Wiccans continues to remain somewhat blurry, but to reiterate: not all witches are Wiccans, and not all Wiccans are witches. Some people will practice witchcraft and subscribe to the religion of Wicca, and some Wiccans will follow the religious beliefs but not practice the rituals or spell work. The rest of this book will focus on both the religious and magickal aspects of Wicca, and as the reader, you are welcome to take them both on board, or just one, or none. It's all up to you.

Chapter 2: Beliefs

As with any other religion, Wicca is centered around a core set of beliefs that inform Wiccan rituals, practices, and daily life.

The Goddess and the God

The Goddess and the God go by many different names. You may hear them being referred to as the Lord and the Lady, the Deities, the Sun God, and the Triple Goddess, to name just a few. In essence, Wiccans believe in a dual deity that is one half Goddess and one half God. It is important to note that believing in a deity does not necessarily mean believing that there is an ancient man in the sky controlling us and judging everything we do. The concept of a God or Goddess can be described as a mystery of being that transcends all other things. Placing this "mystery of being" onto a deity—in this case the Goddess and the God— simply gives us somewhere to direct our beliefs and our energy.

Being a dual deity, the Goddess and the God are two halves of a whole. They exist separately, but they work in harmony with each other. One cannot exist without the other, just like yin and yang or day and night. Wiccans believe that the deity is the original feminine and masculine force that makes all of life possible and is, therefore, present in all people and all things.

The Goddess is connected to the power of the moon, and just as the moon has three phases, the Goddess has three faces: the Maiden, the Mother, and the Crone. The God, then, is connected to the power of the sun and also has three faces: the Green Man, the Horned God, and the Sage. As the year goes by, the Goddess and the God undergo transformations and guide us—and each other—through our own personal transformations.

The Maiden

The Maiden is connected to the crescent moon. She represents new beginnings and new directions. The Maiden is filled with hope, optimism, and a sense of naivete that comes with youth and inexperience. She has choices ahead of her and is full of excitement for what is to come.

The Mother

The Mother is connected to the full moon. She represents existence at its most fertile in every aspect of life, including the mind, the body, and the spirit. The mother is full of creativity, sexuality, and stability. She is nurturing to those around her, be they humans, animals, or plant life. She encourages growth.

The Crone

The Crone is connected to the new moon, sometimes also called the dark or the waning moon. She represents experience, wisdom, and knowledge. She has lived, nurtured, and made choices, and she is now in a position to reflect and advise. The Crone can see both the past and future and is at the threshold of an end and a new beginning.

The Green Man

The Green Man is all about growth and promise. He is young and represents spring, a time for rebirth. He is filled with enthusiasm for the journey ahead and the choices he is about to be faced with.

The Horned God

The Horned God represents fertility, virility, and strength. He is filled with determination and is ready to put his ideas into action by whatever means necessary.

The Sage

The Sage, just like the Crone, represents wisdom, knowledge, and experience. The Sage is a mentor for those around him, and he offers time for reflection and consideration before once again beginning a new journey.

The Power of Nature and the Elements

Believing in the power and divinity of nature is at the root of all Pagan beliefs and, therefore, also the root of Wicca. As explained above, Wicca states that the Goddess and the God were the original forces that created life and are present in all things. That means that all things, big and small, are physical manifestations of the deity and are, in turn, sacred and should be treated as such. It is believed that the Goddess gave birth to all things and receives them again in death.

In addition to this belief is the knowledge that, before the Industrial Revolution and the age of Enlightenment came about and changed the way so many people lived, our ancestors only had nature to guide them through their daily lives. From navigation and shelter, to food and medicine, through to light and heat, ancient civilizations had to harness the power of the earth to survive. Simply put, humans and nature worked in tandem to keep each other happy and healthy. Although in contemporary life technology has made our reliance on nature much less urgent, Wiccans still believe in working in tandem with nature to not only survive, but to thrive.

If the deity is present in nature, then nature has the divine power to guide us through our lives. This power should not only be respected and cared for, but utilized and further energized through our Wiccan practices.

This divine energy that is spread throughout the earth can be divided into four main elements: fire, earth, air, and water. Wiccans harvest these elements in order to give power to their rituals and to inform their practice. Wiccans also acknowledge the existence of a fifth element, the element of the spirit. These elements work together to create the life around us. Just like the Goddess and the God, the elements exist separately but work together. Again, one cannot exist without the other. If just one element were to disappear, the world as we know it would no longer exist. The elements all possess their own unique energy that can be harvested and brought into a Wiccan's magick.

Fire

Fire represents passion and courage. It has a forward and transformative energy. It is masculine, fierce, and strong. It can sometimes also represent anger and danger. Fire is used in rituals and spell work to represent itself.

Earth

Earth as an element is feminine, solid, and stable. It is in everything around us. Anything we can see, touch, taste, and smell contains some of the earth. To represent earth in their rituals, Wiccans use rocks, crystals, and salt.

Air

Air represents creativity and communication. It is light, ever-changing, and masculine. It represents our voice, or our innermost thoughts, as well as art and creative passion. In rituals, air is represented by feathers or incense.

Water

Water is representative of dreams and visions. It is mystical, feminine, cleansing, and healing. Like fire, water also has a forward and transformative energy, but it is a lot slower and more controlled. Water is used in rituals to represent itself.

Spirit

The element of spirit does not take one form. It is a personal element that represents the divine element in the world. It balances and connects the four other elements and is represented in rituals and spell work by the Wiccan themselves.

The Wiccan Rede

The Wiccan Rede is a set of moral codes that Wiccans live by in both their religious practice and their daily life. It can be found in the form of a long poem, and Wiccans often write it down at the start of their Book of Shadows (which we will cover in Chapter 5). The origins of the Rede are somewhat disputed. Some people believe that Gerald Gardner wrote it, but the first recorded version of it is attributed to Doreen Valiente, who was a member of Gardner's coven, in 1964. It is also believed that the full version—known as the Long Rede—was actually written in 1974 by a woman named Phyllis 'Gwen' Thompson. The full version of this Long Rede is below, but the Wiccan Rede is generally considered to be just the final line of this poem.

Bide the Wiccan Laws we must In Perfect Love and Perfect Trust.

Live and let live. Fairly take and fairly give.

Cast the Circle thrice about to keep the evil spirits out.

To bind the spell every time let the spell be spake in rhyme.

Soft of eye and light of touch, speak little, listen much.

Deosil go by the waxing moon, chanting out the Witches' Rune.

Widdershins go by the waning moon, chanting out the baneful rune.

When the Lady's moon is new, kiss the hand to her, times two.

When the moon rides at her peak, then your heart's desire seek.

Heed the North wind's mighty gale, lock the door and drop the sail.

When the wind comes from the South, love will kiss thee on the mouth.

When the wind blows from the West, departed souls will have no rest.

When the wind blows from the East, expect the new and set the feast.

Nine woods in the cauldron go, burn them fast and burn them slow.

Elder be the Lady's tree, burn it not or cursed you'll be.

When the Wheel begins to turn, let the Beltane fires burn.

When the Wheel has turned to Yule, light the log and the Horned One rules.

Heed ye flower, Bush and Tree, by the Lady, blessed be.

Where the rippling waters go, cast a stone and truth you'll know.

When ye have a true need, hearken not to others' greed.

With a fool no season spend, lest ye be counted as his friend.

Merry meet and merry part, bright the cheeks and warm the heart.

Mind the Threefold Law you should, three times bad and three times good.

When misfortune is enow, wear the blue star on thy brow.

True in love ever be, lest thy lover's false to thee.

Eight words the Wiccan Rede fulfill: An ye harm none, do what ye will.

An Ye Harm None, Do What Ye Will

This phrase is the moral code that all Wiccans live by. At first glance, it could be understood as translating to "do no harm." While this is kind of true, it is not the true focus of the Wiccan Rede. Of course, doing no harm—to yourself or others—is a key component of Wicca. It should be a key component to most people's lives. However, the word that truly informs a Wiccan's practice is the word 'will.'

We all know what a 'want' is. I 'want' a piece of cake; you 'want' your friend to get better; we 'want' to be rich. Your want will inform your rituals and spell work, as it will indicate your end goal. Your 'will' is the power inside of you that helps you reach this end goal. Your will is an energy inside of you that will direct you onto the path that you are meant to follow. Focusing on your internal will challenges a Wiccan to act according to their highest purpose. Assuming the Wiccan has tuned in to the divine power of nature and the elements, their will is what directs them to the end goal that is meant for them. If you focus on your will—not just your want—your actions will all stem from a spiritual place, and you will be in harmony with nature and the deity.

Threefold Law

In Wicca, there is no one to tell you what you can and cannot do. If you will harm onto an ex, there won't be someone to come and stop you. However, Wiccans believe in the Threefold Law. This law states that whatever you put out into the world will come back to you three times over. So, if you will something good, good will come back to you. The same goes for negative intentions and energy. The "three times" rule doesn't necessarily mean that three good things or three bad things will happen. Instead, it means that the energy that comes back to you will be three times that which you put out into the universe.

Wicca is all about you and your choices. Your choices will ultimately impact the rhythm of your life. So, if it doesn't harm anyone, follow your will. If it harms anyone, be ready for your will to take you somewhere unpleasant.

Other Beliefs

By nature, Wicca is a collection of practices and beliefs borrowed from other religious systems and stitched together to build a unique craft. With the four main beliefs outlined above acting as the base, many Wiccans will incorporate other beliefs into their religion in order to further inform their practice. The ones listed below are just a few of them.

Reincarnation, the Afterlife, and Animism

Wiccans believe in an afterlife, but it is not as specific as concepts such as "heaven and hell" in Christianity. Essentially, believing in the afterlife just confirms that our lives do not end once we pass away, but that our souls or spirits move on to a new place. This may be the final resting place for our souls, or it could be a sort of "waiting room" as our soul journeys from one life to the next. Many Wiccans also believe in the notion of reincarnation. Whether you believe that someone will come back as a plant, an animal, or as a new person, believing in reincarnation is a logical extension of the birth/death/rebirth cycle that is present in the deities (and in nature, since the deities are present in nature). Finally, the notion of animism recognizes that all living beings on the planet have a soul or spirit, not just humans. From cats to leaves to volcanoes, anywhere the deity is present will follow the birth/death/rebirth cycle.

Divination

Divination is the art of inviting messages from the universe's natural energy and the ability to read these messages. Wiccans generally use divination to look toward the future and seek answers to pressing questions or guidance on making big and important decisions. There are several methods one can opt for when practicing divination, but amongst the most common ones are: tarot, rune stones, tasseography (reading tea leaves), and palmistry. Divination is an occultist skill that is not exclusive to Wicca, but it is an easy skill to pick up by those interested in trying magick.

Astrology

If Wiccans believe that there is a divine power in all natural things from the sun to a grain of sand, then, naturally, this divine power will also exist in the stars and the planets. Astrology is much more than just understanding one's Zodiac chart, although that does come into play here. Rather, Wiccans believe that the positions of the stars and planets will have an effect on our daily lives, from personal decisions to worldwide events. This alignment will then affect your magickal practice and the rituals you choose to perform at a certain time in the year. Additionally, the position of the stars and planets on the day you were born will affect your inner energy and the energy that you put into your practice on a daily basis.

Numerology

Finally, numerology is the belief that all numbers have a spiritual or magickal energy. Every person has a specific number based on their date of birth and the letters in their name, and this number will then affect their energy. Some Wiccans will choose to change their name, picking a new one based on the magickal properties related to the numbers. The correspondence between letters and numbers is as follows:

- 1 = A, J, S
- 2 = B, K, T
- 3 = C, L, U
- 4 = D, M, V
- 5 = E, N, W
- 6 = F, O, X
- 7 = G, P, Y
- 8 = H, Q, Z
- 9 = I, R

You can choose a number that is relevant to you, such as your birth date, or just a number that you feel particularly drawn toward. You would then narrow this date down to a single number. If, for example, your birthday was 08/19/1996, you would go 8+1+9+1+9+9+6 = 43 and then, 4+3 = 7. So, you would choose a letter corresponding to the number 7 to start your new Wiccan name, such as Grace, Pan, or Yule.

You could also just also take your favorite numbers and try to create a unique combination to correspond to a word. So, if you were a fan of the numbers 1, 3, and 7, you could try and create a name that incorporates some of the letters A, J, S, C, I, U, G, P, and Y. Sage, Jack, and Gypsy are three names that could work in that instance.

However you choose to establish your numeric energy, it then manifests in the form of personality traits and life experiences, similar to aspects of astrology. Numbers are also a significant aspect of Wiccan rituals and spells.

Chapter 3: Myths and Misconceptions

Before moving any further in our beginner Wiccan journey, it would be beneficial to pause for a brief moment and have a think about some common myths and misconceptions that surround Wicca. Some of these misconceptions have already been touched on in the first two chapters of this book, and some might seem obvious, but regardless, it is useful to remind ourselves what other people might be thinking about us and why these things they think are most definitely untrue. That is not to say you should go shouting in the faces of people to remind them what Wicca is, but rather use this information to support calm and educated conversations.

Wicca Is Witchcraft

Okay, so actually this first one is kind of true. Sometimes. But not every time.

Wicca is a religious practice that draws from folk traditions, including witchcraft. However, not every person that practices witchcraft abides by Wiccan beliefs, and not every person that identifies as a follower of the Wiccan religion will participate in the magickal or witchcraft aspects of it.

Only Females Can Be Wiccans

This is absolutely not the case; people of any gender can practice Wicca. While the religion has a heavy focus on the feminine energy in humans and in nature, that energy does not exist exclusively in females. The dual energy of the deity—which is feminine and masculine—is present in all of us.

Wicca Is Exclusive

Following on from the previous point, Wicca does not exclude anyone from practicing the religion. People of all genders, races, orientations, beliefs, and backgrounds can practice.

Wicca is also not an exclusive religion in the sense that it can be practiced alongside other religions. You can be a Wiccan and a Buddhist, or Christian, or agnostic. You can even incorporate beliefs and practices from other religions into your Wiccan craft.

Wiccans Are Satanists

Wicca is based on pre-Christian beliefs and practices, so it doesn't even acknowledge the existence of Satan. This misconception probably arose because of the negative connotations attached to the pentagram symbol, which is used in Wicca. The pentagram has gained a bad reputation because it is often misrepresented in pop culture and mass media as being a Satanist symbol. While Satanism does incorporate the pentagram, the symbol itself is not a negative one. The pentagram simply represents the five elements: fire, air, water, earth, and spirit. With the top triangle of the star pointing upwards, the pentagram represents a feminine energy, and when it is inverted, it represents a masculine one. That's it. It is only a Satanic symbol when used by Satanists, and Wiccans are not Satanists.

Wicca Is an Ancient Religion

As we discovered in Chapter 1, Wicca was only really started in the 1940s and 1950s. It does draw on elements from ancient religions and traditions, but as a religion itself, it is not ancient.

Wiccans Use Animal Sacrifices

This one might seem obvious considering everything we have learned about how Wiccans look at nature, but they definitely do not include animal sacrifices in their rituals. Animals may be alluded to with symbols, but a Wiccan would never cause harm to an animal for their practice.

On Accepting the Faith

Because of the misconceptions surrounding Wicca and witchcraft, it can sometimes be scary to tell people about your religion. Some Wiccans use the phrase "coming out of the broom closet" to indicate that they have started to tell people that they are practicing Wicca. However, the response to this "coming out" might not always be a positive one. Here are some things you can do to make this process easier:

- Educate both others and yourself. If you know as much as possible about Wicca, the morals, and the roots of the practice, it will be easier to explain what you are doing to people who might think of scary ladies flying around on brooms when you use the word 'witch.'

- Focus on the "nature-based religion" aspect of the practice. Everyone experiences and understands the power of the natural world, even if they don't consider it to be a divine entity.

- Put yourself first. Making the choice to practice Wicca is a personal decision, so you do not need anyone else's approval to practice. Of course, it would be ideal if the people who are nearest and dearest to you were respectful of your faith, but above all, you are choosing to practice Wicca for yourself and nobody else.

Chapter 4: Picking a Path

So far, we've only really covered tenets of Gardnerian Wicca, the first form of organized Wicca. Yet, as we have also covered, Wiccan practices and beliefs take on many different forms. While they all follow the basic Wiccan beliefs (the deities, the power of nature, and the Wiccan Rede), there are different types of Wicca that each focus on different specific elements.

For example, not all Wiccans will choose to praise the Triple Goddess and the Horned God. Some Wiccans may recognize deities in other forms and from other religions or mythologies, but they believe in the power of a deity in some way. Some Wiccans don't practice magick at all. Some Wiccans will only practice magick when surrounded by other Wiccans.

Different Wiccan paths will also look at the importance of initiation rituals in a different way, which we will also discuss briefly in this chapter.

Types of Wicca

We won't discuss Gardnerian Wicca here because we essentially already have, but just know that it was the first organized form of Wicca and often offers a basis for different types of Wicca.

Alexandrian

This is perhaps the first variation on Wicca to exist after the establishment of Gardnerian Wicca. It was started in the UK in the 1960s by Alex and Maxine Sanders and is very much the same as Gardnerian Wicca, save for two key differences. The first is a focus on gender polarity, which means recognizing a distinct difference between male and female energies in deities and in practitioners. The second is that Alexandrian is considered to be "less strict" than Gardnerian Wicca in its beliefs and rituals. The Alexandrian approach to religion and witchcraft is basically "if it works, use it." Alexandrian covens meet on the full moon, the new moon, and the Sabbat holidays.

Celtic/Faery

Celtic Wicca takes the base principles of all Wicca and incorporates—as the name suggests—elements of Celtic mythology, such as the deities and seasonal festivals. Celtic Wicca teaches an intense love and respect for the earth and focuses on the magickal properties of plants, stones, herbs, trees, and so on. Celtic Wicca also acknowledges the existence of 'fae,' which are magickal creatures such as fairies, gnomes, and sprites.

Faery Wicca is an offshoot of Celtic Wicca that focuses solely on the existence of fae in place of any other deities. Both of these types of Wicca can be practiced solitarily, and you can self-initiate into the practice.

Seax

Seax Wicca is not about sex. This is a Wiccan path that is inspired by Anglo-Saxon pagan practices, beliefs, and iconography. Seax Wicca was founded in the USA in the 1970s by Raymond Buckland and was the first type of Wicca to be practiced in America. Buckland's book *The Tree: Complete Book of Saxon Witchcraft* is considered to be the scripture followed by all Seax Wiccans. They also acknowledge and praise the Triple Goddess and the Horned God, but refer to them as Freya and Woden, respectively. Seax Wicca is a traditionally coven-based practice with High Priests and Priestesses elected democratically on a yearly basis. It can, however, be practiced as a solitary craft too.

Dianic

Dianic Wicca is a feminist branch of Wicca that is for the most part reserved for female Wiccans. It is essentially the same as Gardnerian and Alexandrian Wicca, but it gives additional focus to the Goddess and the earth's female energy. The main deity they praise is the Roman goddess Diana the Hunter, and they often practice meditation and visualization as a coven, alongside their spell work. Traditionally, only women practice Dianic Wicca, but there is an offshoot of this path known as McFarland Dianic Wicca, which accepts practitioners of either gender.

Odyssean

Inspired by the epic Greek poem *The Odyssey* by Homer, this path emphasizes the notion of one's life being a spiritual journey. Odyssean Wicca is an interesting one because it is one of the only Wiccan religions to provide public ministry. That means that anyone who wishes to could attend services, rituals, and training, even if they are not initiated into the craft. However, it does not recognize the idea that people can practice on their own. It has a very intense focus on training, initiation, and degrees. You can attend a service or ritual if you are interested, but you cannot practice without the proper training and initiation.

Another interesting aspect of the practice is that Odyssean Wicca is a multi-pantheon devotional polytheism practice. What this means is that they believe that all the Gods and Goddesses from all ancient pantheons and beliefs are real and exist as separate entities. Odyssean Wiccans are encouraged to pick a small number of deities to relate to and focus on in their personal practice and rituals.

Eclectic

The word 'eclectic' means something that draws on inspiration from various sources, and that is exactly what Eclectic Wicca is. This is currently the most popular Wiccan path, and those that practice it will pick and choose the beliefs, rituals, and deities that they most identify with. Some Eclectic Wiccans will come together to form an Eclectic Coven, but it is definitely a practice that is most popular amongst solitary Wiccans.

Other Paths

Some other Wiccan paths that we haven't discussed here include: Green Wicca, Shaman Wicca, Afro-Wicca, Draconic Wicca, Georgian Wicca, and Church-based Wicca, to name just a few. Of course, there are new paths being developed constantly as more and more people begin their journey into Wicca and forge new paths with fellow Wiccans. It is important to remember that there is no 'right' or 'wrong' way to practice Wicca. The 'right' way is the way that makes you feel comfortable.

Covens and Initiations

For most of its history, Wicca has been practiced in covens, usually in secret. A coven is a group of witches or Wiccans that practice together and follow the same beliefs and teachings. Solitary witches and Wiccans have naturally always existed, but before the information was so widely available, the easiest way to learn about witchcraft and Wicca was from people who already practiced the craft. Since witchcraft—or anything that is perceived as it—was often seen as a taboo and wrong, it wasn't always easy to join a coven. You had to know the coven existed in the first place, and you often had to be invited or accepted into the coven by existing members in the form of an initiation.

Sometimes, you would have to undergo some training and lessons before being initiated, in order to make sure you really know what you're getting into and what the coven's beliefs and practices are. Initiation rituals will differ from coven to coven, and sometimes, you might have to go through several initiations as you progress in your practice. A coven will often pick a specific Sabbat or Esbat as the date for any initiations based on the deities they praise or the energy that they wish to channel.

Is Joining a Coven Necessary?

To put it simply, no, it isn't.

Nowadays, most Wiccans practice on their own anyway. Once you have identified aspects of Wicca that you are interested in, you are essentially ready to begin your practice. The important thing is that you feel comfortable with what you're doing and feel safe in the space you are practicing in. If you wish to self-initiate, you could identify a particular Pagan holiday as the day to start your practice and a specific deity whom you could direct your energy toward.

If you have other Wiccan friends, you could start your own Eclectic Coven and practice together, assuming your beliefs and interests align. Alternatively, you could find yourself a 'circle,' which is the more casual version of a coven. Think of a circle as more of a discussion group, like a book club, but for Wicca. You could meet up with your circle to discuss new things you have learned, write spells together, and maybe even experiment with some magick if you feel comfortable.

If you don't know any other Wiccans but want to find people to practice with, it's not as hard to find covens and circles as you may think. You could either attend Pagan festivals or spiritual stores in your area and speak to the organizers; they might be able to direct you to groups of practicing witches and Wiccans.

Of course, thanks to the magic of technology, you could also find an online coven or circle to join. Many online forums, websites, and Techno-Wiccans using platforms such as Facebook and YouTube will often provide support for new Wiccans. They will sometimes also lead online group rituals, which you can follow along with from your home.

Chapter 5: The Wheel of the Year

The Pagan calendar did not go by months because, when it was created, months weren't a thing yet. Instead, their calendar took the shape of a circle or a wheel. The Wheel of the Year is divided into four quarters, one to mark each season. Wiccans follow the Wheel of the Year to inform their practice, and they celebrate key dates as religious holidays. The Wiccan calendar can be divided into two separate groups of holidays: Sabbats and Esbats. The Sabbats are marked on the Wheel of the Year, but the Esbats aren't. However, many Wiccans will refer to a Second Wheel in order to keep track of the full moons.

Throughout the four seasons, the Wheel tells a mythical story about the relationship between the Goddess and the God; the God, as the Sun, is born, grows strong, and ultimately dies in order to be reborn again. It also follows the agricultural cycles that were crucial for the survival of rural life and communities. The Esbats do the same to follow the journey of the moon and the Goddess, as it journeys between crescent, full, and dark moon.

The Sabbats

The Sabbats are Pagan holidays that all Wiccans celebrate. These holidays follow the change in seasons and the journey of the sun around the earth. They are dedicated to the masculine deity in the form of the Sun God. Since they are linked to the change in seasons, the dates on which these holidays are celebrated vary depending on if you are in the northern or southern hemisphere.

Based on how high or low the sun is in the sky, some Sabbats are considered 'greater' or 'lesser' because of the amount of energy it gives us. Below is a list of every Sabbat, the dates on which they are celebrated in both hemispheres, and a brief look at things you could do to celebrate the holiday.

Yule (lesser Sabbat)

- This is also known as the winter solstice.
- It falls on December 20-23 (north) and the same days in June (south).
- This is when the sun reaches the southernmost point in the sky, so it is the year's shortest day and longest night.
- Yule is a celebration of light amidst a time of darkness, as after this, the days become longer and brighter.
- It is a time to prepare for renewal and new beginnings, and many Wiccans will use this time to plan for the year ahead.
- The festival of Yule is actually the Pagan precursor to the Christian holiday of Christmas, and many Yule celebrations are similar to Christmas ones. During Yule, you can use seasonal herbs, plants, and scents in your rituals and to decorate your altar. Some examples are pine, ivy, mistletoe, holly, cinnamon, cloves, and nutmeg.

Imbolc (greater Sabbat)

- This is also known as Brigid's Day or Candlemas.
- It falls on February 2nd or August 2nd.

- On this day, we celebrate the earth beginning to warm up. It is not quite spring yet, but we are also no longer in the depths of winter.
- Imbolc is a time to clean and cleanse our spaces and our energies, as we prepare for new life to populate the earth.
- This is a popular time for initiations, either self-initiation for solitary Wiccans or into eclectic covens that don't necessarily have a specific day for initiation.
- Ingredients that you can use for rituals at this time include wildflowers, poppyseeds, sunflower seeds, and oats.

Ostara (lesser Sabbat)

- This is also referred to as the spring equinox.
- It falls on March 19-22 or the same days in September.
- At this point, day and night are perfectly balanced and equal in length, so it is a good time to practice balance in our lives too.
- Ostara is all about fertility and growth, as well as care and nurturing. This can mean in animals and nature, as well as in ourselves. It is a good time to check in on your progress and reflect on any practices that might not have been given enough attention.
- The goddess Ostara is often represented in the form of a hare, and this time is dedicated to celebrating the fertility of farm animals, so images of eggs, lambs, and rabbits are extremely popular (similar to during Easter).
- Some herbs, plants, and scents that will be beneficial to rituals at this time include lemon, lilies, strawberries, rose, and lavender.

Beltane (greater Sabbat)

- This is also known as May Day.
- It falls on April 30 to May 1 or on the same days in October and November.
- Beltane happens at the peak of spring and is all about fertility, sexuality, and passion.
- This is a particularly Pagan festival, and many non-Wiccan cultures will celebrate May Day by dancing around a maypole that is considered to be a phallic symbol.
- Beltane celebrates fertility and sexuality in people and the love that brings them together, but it also celebrates the fertility of the earth and the gifts that it gives us. For this reason, you can use any seasonal flowers and leaves you can access in your rituals and at your altar.
- Other popular ingredients are vanilla, paprika, jasmine, and oats.

Litha (lesser Sabbat)

- This is also celebrated as Midsummer or the summer solstice.
- It falls on June 20-24 or the same days in December.
- As it marks the beginning of summer, Litha takes place on the longest day and shortest night of the year. On this day, we celebrate the light being at its peak before we return to the dark in the coming months.
- Litha comes just before the harvest of crops.

- Since the sun is at its peak, this also means it has the strongest energy at this time, so perform any rituals that require lots of energy, such as dreamwork.
- Litha is a perfect time to work with fae, as they will also be out and about to enjoy the sun!
- At your altar and in rituals, you can use citrus, sage, paprika, and honey.

Lammas

- This is also called Lughnasadh.
- It falls on August 1 or the same day in February.
- This is a celebration of the harvest and all the gifts that the earth has provided us with.
- Lammas is a great time to make your own broom with the leftover corn, reed, or wheat from the harvest.
- Bread and baking is a key part of celebrating the harvest as a way to say thank you for nature's bounty.
- If possible, try to use homegrown and local produce, both in your daily meals, as well as in your rituals and spell work during this time.

Mabon

- This occurs on the autumn equinox.
- It falls on September 21-24 or the same days in March.
- During Mabon, the day and night are once again equal, and after this, we begin to lose the light. We use this time to say thank you to summer and the sun for the energy and produce that it has provided us with.

- This is a good time to tie up any loose ends as we approach winter and the end of the harvest season. Popular spells during Mabon will be cleansing and preparation spells for your house or personal space.
- At your altar and in rituals, you should try to use the leaves, pines, and acorns that fall naturally from the trees during autumn.

Samhain

- This is sometimes also referred to as Halloween.
- It falls on October 31 and November 1 or on April 30 and May 1.
- This is the final Sabbat on the Wheel of the Year and a time for celebration before the arrival of winter.
- During Samhain, the veil between the realms of the living and the dead is at its thinnest, so it is a good time to practice spell work that aims to contact the dead.
- It is a time to celebrate our loved ones who have passed and to recognize that there is no life without death, just as there is no light without dark.
- Samhain is also a good time to practice divination.
- Popular foods at this time are corn, apples, and pumpkin. In your rituals, you can use rosemary, mint, cinnamon, and garlic.

The Esbats

The Esbats are celebrated roughly every 29 or 30 days, in conjunction with the full moon each month. There are 12 Esbats, one for every month. Just as the Sabbats praise the energy of the sun and the masculine deity, the Esbats do the same for the moon and the feminine. The names of these moons will vary based on the Wiccan path you follow, and they all have several names, so don't be surprised if you see them being referred to as something else in other sources. Really, knowing the name of the moon is not as important as knowing what it stands for and how to celebrate it.

January

- The Cold Moon
- Focus on promoting individuality and shaping your own unique Wiccan practice.
- Pay attention to communication and use your spell work to encourage better communication with yourself, your deities, and the people you encounter on a daily basis.

February

- The Quickening Moon
- This is a time to look ahead and make plans.
- February's moon will promote divination and reaching out to the spiritual side of life in search of signs.

March

- The Storm Moon
- Focus on your temperament during this moon, and practice patience in your rituals and spell work.
- Use this time to reconcile any damaged bonds in your personal life, and maybe offer up an apology to someone you have wronged.

April

- The Wind Moon
- The energy of April's moon will aid you in the manifestation of your goals, so meditation and visualization will be effective this month.
- It is also a good time to focus on courage and any evidence of stubbornness that might be holding you back from reaching your goals.

May

- The Flower Moon
- Use your spell work and rituals to focus on your potential and encourage growth. This could be either in a particular skill or any elements of your personality that may be lacking maturity.
- May's moon will also give power to fertility.

June

- The Sun Moon
- Take a look at where change of any kind is needed in your life and direct your energy toward it.
- June is about transformation in any form; you should manifest or banish, increase or decrease.

July

- The Blessing Moon
- If you have had any plans sitting idly, July is a time to get them moving.
- Use your spell work and rituals to promote productivity in the coming winter months.

August

- The Corn Moon
- This is a time to clean and cleanse, both your personal energy and your physical space.
- Prepare for a time of solitude and encourage a peaceful approach to the colder months.

September

- The Harvest Moon
- Focus on building strong foundations in your relationships with everyone in your life (including your relationship with yourself).
- This is a time to promote love of all kinds.

October

- The Blood Moon
- Encourage balance and justice with your rituals and spell work, and focus on elements of your life that seem to be thrown off-kilter.
- October's moon will give strength to divination practices and make communication with the spirit world easier.

November

- The Mourning Moon
- Release any emotion that has been holding you back from either reaching personal goals or being your best self.
- Banish any negative energy taking over your mind or your space.

December

- The Long Night Moon
- Prepare yourself for the coming year, and focus on balancing your inner and outer lives.
- Be ready for external truths to be brought to light, as others also prepare for the coming year.

A Note on the Sun and the Moon

The Sun and the Moon are very prominent figures in Wicca. Obviously, they are considered to be representative of the God and Goddess, but if you choose to not align your Wiccan practice with the existence of these deities, there is still benefit in observing the Sabbats and Esbats. On a purely physical level, the sun and the moon have an essential effect on the way our earth works, and acknowledging the natural powers of the universe is at the heart of any Wiccan or Pagan religion.

Additionally, marking off specific dates in your calendar to observe as holidays is never a bad thing. Wiccan Sabbats are a time for celebration in any capacity. You can celebrate by throwing a big party full of music and cakes, or you can just take a moment to light a candle and reflect on your journey up until this point.

The Esbats are not considered holidays, but rather serve as markers to guide your practice. As you progress in your Wiccan journey, you will learn how each different moon will affect your practice. Until then, you can just check in with our list if you are looking for some inspiration or a simple suggestion as to what kind of magick to focus on next.

While you are still figuring out your own path and practicing as a beginner Wiccan, try not to get too caught up on the name of each moon or the specific ways to celebrate each Sabbat. Just use the Wheel of the Year and the journey of the moon to help you give some structure to your practice.

Chapter 6: Practicing Wicca

Wiccan ritual magick comes in various forms, including but not limited to spell work, divination, potion making, and mental magick such as telepathy. Chapter 7 of this book will introduce you to the basics of Wiccan magick, as well as a couple of beginner spells for you to try your hand at. However, before we head over there, it's important to get a basic understanding of the tools you might need to have on hand.

Tools

The below list might sound like a lot of things to consider before starting your own journey, but it is useful to know what you might want to incorporate into your own practice. These tools are all traditional and useful in Wiccan magick, but they are not all necessary. Additionally, getting your hands on some of these tools is as simple as buying a new cup or picking up a stick from your garden.

Let's break things down and start by looking at the key tools.

Athame

An athame is a sword or ritual knife, but it is never used to actually cut anything. Your athame is used for directing energy in rituals, such as casting a circle or cutting something metaphorically if you are working a spell to cut a bond or free something. It generally has a black handle and an inscription on the blade (which can be blunt). It can be made of wood, stone, crystal, or metal, and you can decorate it as you wish. It is often suggested to keep a separate knife at your altar to use for the cutting of herbs and rope.

Wand

If you are not comfortable using an athame in your ceremonies, a wand serves the same purpose. Typically made of wood or stone with a tapered cylinder shape that is wider at the end that you hold, it can also be decorated and inscribed. Choosing between a wand and an athame is generally a matter of personal preference. However, if you choose to work with fae in your craft, a wand is suggested.

Chalice

A chalice is a cup that is used specifically at your altar and only for Wiccan ceremonies. It can be an ornate, expensive goblet or a simple mug from the thrift store. The important thing is that it hasn't been used for anything other than Wiccan ceremonies. The contents of the chalice—most often wine or water—are usually used as symbolic offerings for the deities.

Cauldron

A pot that is used to hold and burn items, such as water, oils, papers, and herbs. It is generally made of cast iron and stands on three legs, so a source of heat can be placed underneath. However, any sort of pot or container can be used as long as it is able to withstand heat. It is very important that your cauldron is thoroughly cleaned after ceremonies, spells, and rituals to avoid contaminating your next ritual.

Broom

No, brooms aren't used by Wiccans—or witches for that matter— as a flying mode of transportation. A broom is used to sweep away negative and unwanted energy from a space before casting a circle. You can make your own broom from wood, twigs, and rope, or you can buy one. If you buy one, be sure to buy one that is made of only organic materials, as synthetic materials, such as glue and plastic, can inhibit the flow of energy.

Candles

Candles are used for a wide variety of things in Wiccan practice. They can be used to represent the element of fire, to represent a specific color's energy, or simply as a source of heat.

Many Wiccans will opt to have two specific candles to represent male and female energies. These candles are placed on the left and right of the altar respectively and are generally a dark color (blue, gray, or red) for the male energy and lighter colors (gold, white, or rose) for the female.

Divination Tools

If you practice divination, it is useful to keep your tools at your altar. These tools can include tarot cards, teacups and leaves, runes, a crystal ball, or a scrying mirror. Divination is an aspect of Wicca that not all Wiccans practice, but it is growing in popularity.

Others

In reality, you can set up your altar to include any of the key tools and elements you use in your practice. Some things, such as water and salt, don't necessarily need to be kept at your altar, but it is more convenient to have them there.

Other items you can keep at your altar include crystals, sage, incense, bells, a pentagram, herbs, statues, pen and paper, essential oils, and your Book of Shadows.

Book of Shadows

A Book of Shadows is a Wiccan hand-written book that contains religious texts, instructions for rituals, information on beliefs and values, and spells to be practiced. In a coven, there will be one collective Book of Shadows that all members will refer to. Members of a coven will sometimes write out their own copies for personal reference, but their own copy won't vary in any way from the one approved by the founders or High Priest or Priestess. A collective Book of Shadows that is passed down in covens and families is sometimes also called a Grimoire.

In eclectic and solitary Wicca, a Book of Shadows is a lot more personal and sometimes acts more like a journal than a sacred text. You can use your Book of Shadows to collect magickal lore that you come across, information on the properties of specific herbs and plants, spells you are learning or working on, and so much more. For eclectic and solitary Wiccans, a Book of Shadows is considered something extremely personal, and there aren't that many rules when it comes to making your own. A good way to start your Book would be to write down a protection spell and the Wiccan Rede—or any other moral code—on the first few pages. After that, you can fill out the rest of it with your own writing and research, as well as some drawings too. You don't need to fill it out all at once; just like a journal, you can add more to your Book of Shadows as you learn and grow in your craft. You should keep your Book of Shadows at your altar with your other Wiccan tools, mostly out of convenience. Your Book of Shadows can obviously be brought out and about with you—again, this is a personal object—but keeping it at your altar means you won't ever forget where it is!

Altars and Circles

We keep saying "at your altar" over and over again, but what does that mean exactly? It is basically a surface that is considered sacred and only used for Wiccan rituals and objects. It can be anything from a large table to a small wall shelf, or even a marked off area of your floor or a shelf inside a cupboard. An altar is used for all forms of Wiccan magick and reflection, and just like the Book of Shadows, it is a very personal aspect of your practice. You can set up and decorate your altar however you like, using any of the tools we just went over and other images and symbols that you consider relevant. An altar can be a permanent setup that is always in place, or you can create a temporary one as and when you need it.

A circle—unlike an altar—is not something that is constantly set up. Casting a circle is generally the first step in any Wiccan ritual, and it includes setting up a perimeter of energy around you before continuing the ritual. Again, we'll go into more detail on this topic in the next chapter, but to provide a general introduction: The circle helps to focus your Wiccan energy and keep it directed to your task at hand. It also keeps any negative or unwanted energy away from you while you work. You can mark out the circle with things like salt, chalk, stones, candles, herbs, or crystals, and as soon as you cast it, until you close it at the end of your ritual, it is considered to be a sacred space. Your circle will usually be cast in front of and around your altar, since both spaces are used in the working of rituals and magick.

Chapter 7: Making Magick

Magick is essentially the ability to manipulate the physical world around you, generally using ritualistic actions. The word 'physical' might be a bit confusing because sometimes magick can produce abstract results, such as a change in feelings. However, these metaphorical changes will affect the physical world and those of us who inhabit it, which is why that word is being used here. To make these manipulations, we need to tap into our will, as discussed in Chapter 2. Focusing on our will and directing it to manipulate the physical world requires a significant amount of energy.

Before you take the next step and give a spell a try, it is important that you understand some basic principles and techniques.

Basic Principles

Energy

The most important thing to know is that the energy you are using is not your own energy. Additionally, this energy is neutral; it is neither positive nor negative. Your will and the way you choose to direct this neutral energy will then affect the outcome of the intended transformation.

Energy exists all around us, in all things and people. This energy is the divine energy that we have discussed earlier in this book and is given to the earth by the deities. Accessing this divine energy takes a certain amount of mental strength. Just like with physical strength, you need to exercise and train it. You also need to warm up to avoid mental strain, meaning you cannot just go straight into a ritual or spell.

Grounding

Before starting a ritual, many Wiccans will begin by practicing something called 'grounding.' There are two aspects to this; the first is to "shake off" negative or unwanted energy, and the second would be to tune in with your surroundings to access the divine energy around you. How you choose to shake off your negative energy is entirely personal. You could actually physically shake it off, do some yoga or physical exercise, or engage in meditation or mindfulness exercises. Even the simple acts of taking a shower or eating something can help you to feel grounded. If you are feeling tired or are lacking your own personal energy, grounding will help you to better access the earth's energy and direct it appropriately.

Shielding

Once you feel grounded, you need to direct your energy correctly. Otherwise, you could end up sending your energy all over the place. To direct this energy, you need to put some boundaries in place, which is also referred to as the act of shielding.

'Shielding' is basically creating a barrier around you while you practice ritual magick, which helps you to control what energies impact your practice. This barrier can be metaphorical—

established by engaging a mental shield against negative influences—or it can be physical. This is where the act of casting a circle comes in. As a quick refresher, Wiccans cast a circle around themselves and their altars as the first step in any magickal ritual. The circle can be fully drawn out on the floor using salt or chalk, or you can simply mark out the four cardinal directions—also called the quarters—with items such as crystals or candles. Marking out the four quarters is important because each direction corresponds to a specific element: east for Air, south for Fire, west for Water, and north for Earth.

Once you've drawn your circle, you will then 'invoke' or 'call' the quarters into action, in order to activate their protective and creative qualities. You can choose to do this by walking around the circle and stopping next to each quarter, pointing to the quarters with your athame or wand, or by performing a mini-ritual at each quarter using a tool that corresponds with the appropriate element. Once you have called the quarters into action, you can also invoke the deities and invite them to join your ritual to support you or to witness your offerings. This can be done by simply using words—poetry or verse—spoken out loud.

Again, how you choose to shield yourself is a matter of personal preference and will also depend on the items and space that you have at your disposal.

Visualization

Finally, visualization is a technique that Wiccans often use to support the direction and flow of their energy.

The idea is that you need to transform your thoughts from words into images because images are generally more impactful and will give your energy more power. If you think of the visual aspect of something—as opposed to just thinking of the name of it—you will have a clearer idea of what you are aiming for. Thinking of what the sea looks like is more effective to your memory than just thinking of the word 'sea.' Visualizing your plant growing is more effective for your growth spell.

In order to strengthen your visualization skills, all you really have to do is train yourself to think in images. Here is an example of an exercise you can carry out to help train your brain.

Hold up something in front of you, like a keychain or this book, and look at it closely. Feel it too. Examine the colors, the textures, how it feels in your hands, what it smells like, and take in all the details you possibly can. Now, put it down, close your eyes, and try to remember those details. Try and recreate the item in your memory, from the shape and color to the weight and smell. When the details fade from your mind's view, open your eyes, and look at it again. How closely did you recreate it?

Repeat this exercise with this object until you feel confident in your ability to visualize it, and then move on to a new one. If you are feeling super confident, you can try to memorize and visualize several objects at once. Then, you can do it with your entire room or a person or animal.

Sample Spells

Now that you have a clear understanding of Wiccan principles, beliefs, and practices, it might be time for you to try your hand at some actual magick. Remember that you do not need to practice magick and witchcraft to practice Wicca; you could simply apply the key religious principles and morals to your day-to-day life. If you do want to give magick a go, though, here are three easy spells you might want to attempt.

These spells and rituals can all be practiced on your own and in your own space, and they require minimal or easy-to-access tools and ingredients.

A Purification Ritual

This ritual is an ideal one to start with. Not only is it easy with minimal tools and ingredients, it also works to purify a new space that hasn't yet been used for witchcraft. This ritual is best performed on the night of a New Moon, as it is an ideal time to mark off new beginnings and prepare for future practice and plans.

For this purification ritual, all you need is:

- water
- sea salt
- a flat dish/saucer
- a teaspoon
- incense of your choice

Fill your saucer with water. Dip the index finger of your dominant hand into the water, and leave it there. While the tip of your finger is submerged in water, visualize a beam of bright light traveling from the top of your head, through your body, and into the water. While focusing on directing that light into your water, recite the following words:

Here do I direct my power,
Through the agencies of the God and the Goddess,

Into this water, that it might be pure and clean
As is my love for the Lord and Lady.

Remove your finger from the dish. Pour one teaspoon of sea salt into the dish and—using the same finger as before—stir it clockwise nine times. As you stir, recite the following three times:

Salt is Life. Here is Life. Sacred and new; without strife.

Now, dip all your fingers into the purified water, and sprinkle it around every corner of your room or the space you are practicing in. These corners include corners inside cupboards and on shelves, not just the corners created by walls. While you are sprinkling, recite the following chant. You could also write your own variation on this chant, if you so wish.

Ever as I pass through the ways, so I feel the presence of the
Gods. I know that in aught I do They are with me.
They abide in me.
And I in them, forever.

No evil shall be entertained, for purity is the dweller within me
and about me. For good do I strive and for good do I live. Love
unto all things.

So mote it be, forever.

Lastly, burn some incense and direct it toward all the corners once more. This incense can be a scent of your choice, perhaps one that calms you or is relevant to the upcoming Sabbat. As you spread the incense around, repeat one of the previous charms (or write your own). After you have completed this ritual—and any others you plan on performing—dispose of the purified water into a plant or somewhere outside.

A Space Blessing Spell

This spell is not that different to the first one in terms of intent, but it is slightly more complex and reaches further than one confined space. The intention with this ritual is to bless a space—such as a room or a whole house—and promote the growth of positive energy within the walls. There are slightly more ingredients required for this spell, but they are all easy to access. The ingredients include:

- fennel
- basil
- peppermint oil
- black salt (or a mixture of coal and salt)
- sage
- water
- a source of fire (a candle, lighter, or match)
- a tea light
- your chalice
- a heat-resistant dish

Begin by placing the tea light on or in your dish, but do not light it yet. Next, place a sprig of fennel, a basil leaf, a dash of peppermint oil, and some black salt onto the tea light to anoint it. Lift your dish and carry it to the entrance of your house (or room). Light the tea light and recite:

This house is good, so not its past, clear this room, let happiness last.

Now, place the dish down on a surface within that room and clap twice. Clapping will work to further get rid of any negative vibrations lingering in the space. Repeat this sequence of chanting and clapping in every room that you wish to bless. When you are done, return to your altar and place the dish down. Do not blow out the tea light, but leave it at the altar to let it burn down. As it burns down, you can stare into the flame and visualize negativity burning away alongside it.

Light your sage and return to the entrance. Walk around the house and into every room that you walked into previously. As the sage burns, recite:

By the powers of Fire and Air, I cleanse this house.

Lastly, fill your chalice with a mixture of water and salt. Return to the entrance, and as we did in the first spell, sprinkle the water in the corners of your space. As you sprinkle, recite:

By the powers of Earth and Water, I cleanse this house.

Finally, return to your altar and recite something along the lines of:

I thank the elements for blessing this house, so mote it be.

Just as before, be sure to dispose of your water in a plant, garden, river, or any other outdoor area.

A Money Charm

If you have tried the above spells and feel comfortable moving on to something more complex, give this money charm a try. Now to be clear, performing this ritual doesn't mean you will automatically come into an unimaginable amount of money. However, it will promote prosperity and abundance that will encourage financial gain.

For this charm, you will need:

- a green candle
- prosperity oil (details on this will follow the ritual)
- a source of fire
- patchouli incense
- something that represents money
- You will also need an object to imbue with this energy. This could be a pendant worn around a chain, a crystal, or something more specific, such as a money clip or a coin.
- If you are anointing an amulet, you need dried mint, patchouli, and a green aventurine.

Anoint your candle with prosperity oil, and then, light it and the incense with the same flame. Place something that is symbolic of money at your altar. This can be a coin, paper note, bank card, or an image representing any of the above.

Anoint your object with prosperity oil. If you are choosing to wear your object as a pendant, pass a silver chain or black chord through it. If your object will take the form of an amulet, place it inside a green bag alongside the mint, patchouli, and aventurine.

Pass your object through the smoke of the incense and the candle, and recite:
Let abundance come to me, allow my dreams to flow. Let me

*give back more than I receive.
So mote it be.*

Take some time to visualize the divine energy passing through the smoke and into your object. Thank your deities if you invoked them at the start of your ritual work.

Prosperity Oil

If you wish to create your own prosperity oil, this is very simple. All you need is:

- a base oil such as olive, grapeseed, or vegetable
- an essential oil such as peppermint or patchouli
- dried mint
- dried patchouli
- cinnamon stick
- allspice (whole)
- a glass bottle that can be closed

Pour the oils and herbs into a bottle, cap it, and shake it. Place the bottle outside or by a window at nighttime to charge under the power of the moon. Shake the bottle every time you use it to ensure all the elements are properly combined.

Conclusion

Well done! You now should have a decent grasp on Wiccan principles and practices. From the origins of the religion to ways to try your hand at magick, we've covered a lot of ground. Seriously though, we have covered a lot, so take some time to congratulate yourself for coming this far. This may just be the start of your journey as a Wiccan, but it was a strong start. You have equipped yourself with enough information and knowledge to kick-start your journey into a whole new faith.

Well done, you.

A Few Things to Remember

If you went into this book totally blind, it's understandable that you might be feeling slightly overwhelmed. Here are some things to do and keep in mind if you feel that way:

- Take your time. You don't need to go straight into daily, complicated practice and rituals. Start by incorporating simple Wiccan morals into your day-to-day actions or by just acknowledging the Sabbats and Esbats as they happen. Maybe even incorporate the relevant ingredients into your meals on the day of the Pagan holidays.

- Read more. Look into the lore and history of deities you feel drawn toward. Learn about the properties possessed by different herbs, stones, and so on. Decide if you want to align with any specific Wiccan path or if you want to create your own Eclectic practice.

- Start your Book of Shadows and carry it around with you. If you have some free time, you can read any notes you have already made, write out some new spells and chants to get familiar with the language, or make lists of things you want to focus on in the coming days.

- Wicca is a personal journey. You can shape and mold it to suit your personal preferences. This is, after all, what Gerald Gardner did when he first established Wicca in the 1950s and what many other Wiccans did after him. If something doesn't feel right or comfortable, you don't have to do it.

- Wicca is not a one-time deal. You can start and stop as you move further through your journey. You can start following certain rules and principles and change the way you practice as you learn more. You can practice Wicca alongside other religions and daily practices if you want to.

- Remember the Wiccan Rede, "An ye harm none, do what ye will." If you ever need to re-ground yourself or rediscover the roots of Wicca, head back over to Chapter 2 in this book and give it a once over to remind yourself why you align with Wicca in the first place and what beliefs you would like to adopt.

So, What Next?

A good question with a simple answer really: Just keep practicing.

However, if you want a more specific answer, we would suggest taking some time now to solidify the key aspects of your beliefs and the path you wish to follow. You could choose to try and follow the specific practices of an established Wiccan path or just decide which elements you want to incorporate into your practice. Again, this is not something that will be set in stone, your practice can—and probably will—change as you learn and grow. Yet, it would be good to identify some starting beliefs, as this will help to give you a sense of direction.

Next, you could try your hand at some more complex spell work. If you search my name on Amazon (Sarah Rhodes), I have books specifically dedicated to spell work that you can purchase! You could also see if you want to give divination a try or do some work with crystals and stones. Once you're feeling comfortable with using witchcraft and performing magickal rituals, you can move on to more complex spells.

I hope you have enjoyed this beginner's guide to Wiccan magick or, at the very least, have gained a better understanding of this fascinating and diverse religion. Thank you for reading. We will leave you with this short prayer of gratitude to you the reader and to the God and Goddess who have guided us as we explored the world of Wicca together.

Lord and Lady, I give thanks, for sun that warms and wind that sings.

You have given me so much, now I give you thanks for all these things.

So mote it be.

Now, go forth and practice (with) kindness.

References

Barrette, E. (2002, March 8). *Spell: gratitude spell.* Llewellyn Worldwide. https://www.llewellyn.com/spell.php?spell_id=651

Bruhun, S. (2020). *Wicca book of spells and witchcraft for beginners.* Andrea Astemio.

Buckland, R. (1995). *Witchcraft from the inside : origins of the fastest growing religious movement in America.* Llewellyn Publications.

Campbell, J. (1988). *The power of myth* [DVD]. *PBS.*

Chamberlain, L. (2020). *Wicca for beginners : A guide to wiccan beliefs, rituals, magic & witchcraft.* Sterling Ethos.

Cougar, M. (2012). *The sacred wheel.* new age & spiritual books.

Nice, H. (2019). *Wicca : a modern guide to witchcraft & magick.* Seal Press.

Raine, A. & Gonzalez, A. (2020). *The essential guide to Wicca for beginners : 52 spells and rituals plus magical history.* Rockridge Press.

Sabin, T. (2006). *Wicca for beginners : fundamentals of philosophy & practice.* Llewellyn Publications.

Van, N., & Vernon, K. (2017). *Practical magic : a beginner's guide to crystals, horoscopes, psychics & spells.* Running Press.

Wigington, P. (2019, April 28). *What's in a magical name for Pagans?* Learn Religions.

https://www.learnreligions.com/your-magical-name-2562872

www.ingramcontent.com/pod-product-compliance
Lightning Source LLC
Chambersburg PA
CBHW070934120626
46546CB00004B/1420